breakfast without tiffany
AN INSPIRATIONAL JOURNEY OF FAITH

*Best wishes
AnnaMaria*

breakfast without tiffany

AN INSPIRATIONAL JOURNEY OF FAITH

ANNA MARIA SPARKS

Mill City Press
Minneapolis, MN

Copyright © 2010 by Anna Maria Sparks

Mill City Press, Inc.
212 3rd Avenue North, Suite 290
Minneapolis, MN 55401
612.455.2294
www.millcitypublishing.com

All rights reserved. No part of this publication may be reproduced, stored in a retrieval system, or transmitted, in any form or by any means, electronic, mechanical, photocopying, recording, or otherwise, without the written prior permission of the author.

ISBN - 978-1-936400-54-6
LCCN - 2010937249

Cover Design & Typeset by Melanie Shellito

Printed in the United States of America

DEDICATION

*To the Holy Trinity, the Father, the Son,
and the Holy Ghost, who especially in my darkest hours never
left my side.*

*To my generous Mother, I'm grateful for your heroic efforts
and relentless energy.*

To my soul mate Jeremiah, for his inspirational love.

*To my beautiful children, Tiffany and Carlo, whose love
for each other took me beyond my own emotions, higher than
my selfishness, closer to God.*

TABLE OF CONTENTS

All Things Begin in Spring 1

La Mama 9

Dancing Up a Storm.....................................13

Premonition 17

Seek and Ye Shall Find...................................25

The Demons of Doubt...................................29

Rescue Me 39

All the King's Horses and All the King's Men.............45

Confrontation 49

All of the Grace and All of the Glory.....................58

About the Author 69

1

ALL THINGS BEGIN IN SPRING

Toronto Star
April 23, 1992
(excerpts from article)

200 DIE AS BLASTS RIP OPEN MEXICO STREETS

Guadalajara, Mexico (Reuters-AP)—The death toll climbed past 200 early today after a series of sewer explosions ripped open streets and flattened buildings in Mexico's second largest city. At least 600 people were injured in yesterday's disaster...

Nine explosions, beginning at 10:30 am, blasted enormous craters and left jagged trenches up to 4 kilometers (2 ½ miles) long in Avenida Gante and other streets in the Reforma district of southeastern Guadalajara. About 1,000 buildings were damaged, many heavily...

Passengers were trapped in a bus that fell into a hole caused by the blast...

Seven hundred rescue workers were searching for victims (last night) of the series of explosions that have devastated the city...

Guadalajara, famed for its Spanish Colonial architecture, is perhaps the stateliest of Mexico's largest cities...

April 22, 1992
4:30 pm

"Raul!" I shouted from the bottom of the stairs. "I'm leaving now."

"Wait, Annamaria," he said frantically. "Where are you going?"

I snarled my mouth and rolled my eyes as I watched him scurry down the marble steps.

"I've told you three times already where I'm going! You don't listen to a single word I say... stop wasting my time, I gotta go and pay this phone bill." With a cocky attitude I snapped at him and braced myself for the repercussions.

"You can go tomorrow, and don't talk to your husband like that!"

He slapped me square across the face. "Now tell me the

real reason why you have to go today. It's due tomorrow, I said—you go and do that tomorrow," he commanded me.

"Why... why wait?" The words I spoke left me with a strange taste in my mouth; I paused to analyze that sensation. Then I resumed with my argument. "Why put things off for tomorrow what you can do today..." The sting of his slap heated my cheek and my temper soared.

"I hate you! You're an idiot! I want a divorce! Why do I need you?" I kept walking as I ran my mouth. He shouted after me.

"Divorce? I'll kill you! I'll throw you off the *baranca* and the coyotes will tear you into pieces...no one will ever find you..."

* * *

Mi Patito Lindo (my lovely duck), a charming yet a tad insulting nickname given to me by one of Mama's friends mostly for my overbite and pouty upper lip, or possibly for my inability to keep my mouth shut. By the time I was twenty-one my teeth had straightened themselves out, I had lost my round face to a distinct European chisel, and my hazel eyes turned blue-green, ignited by my dark olive skin and jet-black hair.

These natural events rendered me more attractive than your average beautiful *Tapatia* (woman of Jalisco), thus making modeling jobs plentiful and leaving us financially abundant. My husband, still an old-fashioned Mexican man, was disturbed by my success. Raul loathed my ego, and there was lots of it.

He would drop the kids off at his mother's as soon as I left for a photo shoot and disappear into the city for days at a time. I would pick them up from Abuelita's house. Our daughter Tiffany's clothes would be disapprovingly changed into a new dress, the stiff itchy ruffly kind, her long beautiful hair slicked up tight in tacky colored bobbles and her hands tied so she wouldn't get dirty.

My toddler, Carlo, was unbathed, untouched, free to roam, like the vagabond dogs on the streets. Cornsilk hair, rosy cheeks, pale skin—a mirror image of da Vinci's creation of an angel—made him easy to spot when he played with all of the other kids.

When Tiffany turned six I brought her with me most everywhere. I plopped her up on the runway with the junior line, and my little kitten tore up the catwalk. A beautiful, bold, tiny dancer, with such natural style and grace.

There was something very adult about my daughter Tiffany. The reflective way she tilted her chin, her still gaze. Calm, mature, a wise old soul destined for greatness. At a very young age she started ballet class—and dance she did! She lived and breathed it, much to Mama's delight. Her sandy brown hair flew behind her as she spun her baby brother around the living room, performing her interpretation of the latest Disney musical.

Raul constantly berated me. "No daughter of mine will be a dancer or a model—that's for whores!"

"But that's what I've been doing my whole life! When we met—when you married me! When I gave you children! Am *I* a whore?!"

He stared at me, without remorse, without regret, with that stupid look on his face. The one you get when you have nothing to say.

Nothing.

The truth is Raul's life was full of regret; this was just one more thing that he wished he had never done, our marriage not withstanding. Just a few years ago he was percussionist with Carlos Santana, but Raul quit the band to start his own musical group and play American rock music. A strange move considering his own background, son of the late Lino Briseno, who played with the original Mariachi Vargas of Guadalajara, who have become immortalized by Mexican cinema. Don Lino brought great honor and pride to the family. The Mariachis are the cornerstone of Mexican culture. Cuisine, Tequila and Music, the very essence of The Republic of Mexico.

Raul's bad judgment haunted him on a daily basis. He was ten years my senior and not aging well. His head of once long blond curly locks, now replaced with rat tails, patchy and unkept. He was thin, too thin, with no more muscle tone. The drugs and alcohol had sucked him dry and he knew it. This added to his ever-growing insobriety. He wallowed in self-pity and I found his presence completely insupportable. On this unmarked day in April, the day before the tragic explosion, Raul was just ending the third decade of his life, and his youth, along with his friends and fans, had abandoned him some years ago.

Still, he held on to his dreams, and onto his beautiful young wife—there was no way Raul would ever give up the one thing that his peers admired about his life, no matter how unhappy we were. He was never going to let me go. And I knew it.

I belonged to him.

I was his possession.

* * *

April 22, 1993, another brilliantly sunny day in bustling city of Guadalajara. It was late in morning and the kids were playing in the pool; the house was too hot that time of day, fortunately.

BOOM BA BA BA!! The earth shook and rumbled under our feet.

A piercing screech...a long hiss...and another...*BOOM!!*

The explosion shocked us. It was a sound we had never heard before, like a sonic boom. Immediately I ran over to my children, physically pulled them out of the water, and continued running to the furthest corner of the yard. I huddled them under my chest and curled over my babies, covering their heads as best as I could. My first instinct was to think it was an earthquake. I had experienced a few of those before. But rapidly analyzing the moment, I realized it could not be a quake. Something else had happened, something horrible. The air filled quickly with dust particles, the squeal of sirens almost drowned out the sounds of people screaming.

"Mommy, what happened?" Tiffany turned to me for answers. Carlo kept a silent watch at the both of us. He did not cry.

"Come on, stay close to me." I picked them both up and walked towards the house. Cautiously I opened the back door. The smoke and dust created a thick black layer on the floor. We shuffled through it, heedfully making our way to the front of the house.

"Where's the door?" Tiffany whispered.

"There it is!" Carlo pointed to the steel door lying on my kitchen countertop.

"How did it get there?" Tiffany's voice shrieked with fear.

With complete composure I told the children, "It must have been an explosion of some kind...we have to leave this house now. We will come back when it's fixed."

They nodded their little heads in comprehension. I tried to downplay the disaster. "It's just a door and a piece of wall, it shouldn't take long to fix."

We headed upstairs and threw a few things in a suitcase.

Raul was shouting our names well before he was in the house.

"What happened?" I mouthed the words carefully, so that he understood and the kids wouldn't hear me.

Raul's face was white, his breath short.

"It's like a war," he described. "Dead people everywhere..." I put my hands over my mouth and sat down. "Telefono Tower...the one you were supposed to go to today...but you went yesterday..." He was babbling, but I understood. "*It's gone!* The whole thing! Gone! Its a hole now...Annamaria... do you understand me? It's just a big hole!" He was shouting with anxiety, shaking all over.

"Was it a bomb? Do you know anything else? What are the people saying?"

"They say it was gas," Raul tried to explain. "Gas in the pipes."

"I don't understand." I began to feel sick. "We have to go to a safe place. Is it all over the city?"

"No, the radio said just Sector Reforma," Raul answered.

I finished tying the shoelaces on Carlo's sneakers, picked up the suitcase, and took a deep breath, doing my absolute best to stay unperturbed.

"Okay, drive us to the Fiesta Americana Hotel on the other side of town."

That was the last time I saw my beautiful house. How quickly materialistic things lose their value in the face of disaster. As I walked with my children beyond the confines of our home, I realized we were lucky to be alive. A house close to ours had sustained far more damage.

"Gloria's place? Are they okay?" I ask.

Raul turned and looked at me as he drove, the expression on his face, the quivering lip, the tears steaming down his face at the death that besieged us.

As we made our way to the north side of town, the

destruction zone was thick with ugliness. At the corner of Revolucion and Independencia Avenue, we witnessed an indisputable demonstration of the pure force of the blast. A three-ton dump truck had been thrown into the air and landed face down on the top of a four-story office building. The next corner, gone, in its place a huge crevice, the perimeter sharply marked with flames; the center of the circle was dark and vast, a huge void, a lifeless abyss. Steel, rubble, and human body parts littered the streets. It was so gruesome. I instructed the children to cover their eyes and try not to look. The images of horror will forever be burned in my mind.

I later learned that the whole disaster could have been avoided. That corrupt bureaucrats, not fate, had been the doom of those poor souls. Someone at Pemex, the company that monopolized gasoline in Mexico, had substituted a cheap defective pipe when they installed their last project. The gasoline then made its way into the city's sewage system and the results were catastrophic. The stench of death was pungent, thick, dark, and frightening.

It was a dangerous time in my life. Danger for my children and myself. An abusive marriage, a volatile environment. I had to find a way out. I was young, successful, and overly confident in my own abilities and mortality. Yet even as I dealt with the moment, the uncertainty, I knew my journey began with a voice—my celestial confidant that summoned me...

"Take your children and get as far away as you can, leave your earthly possessions and run for your life..."

Does not wisdom cry out? And understanding lift up her voice. She takes her stand on top of the high hill.
—Proverbs 8:1

2

LA MAMA

Everyone has a time in their life that, when looked back on, is classified as "that defining moment." You never actually feel it as it happens, but rather it manifests itself as who you will someday be, good or bad, traumatic or simply divine, a moment in time when change is a necessary part of survival.

La Mama, as they called her, was the queen of change, a true Gemini, restless and adventurous. La Mama, an accomplished dancer, choreographer, and businesswomen—and of course mother of four daughters, myself included—had a few monsters in her closet, carefully camouflaged with proficiency.

I do recall coming home one day to our luxurious suburban house viciously and completely vandalized. Confusion and anger rang frantically though the air. In my sister's room were the toys and stuffed animals, a collection of hundreds, all with their heads violently cut off. Someone was going to hurt us. I was told to pack some things, we were moving, now.

I don't ever stress about what happened to me as a child, I just simply have no memory of my childhood. For me, life began at sixteen when we moved to Acapulco.

In my mind, life begins in a dry gray, black, and white, and then magnificently explodes into tropical living color and song.

La Mama landed a glamorous choreographer's position

in an Acapulco nightclub. The Pearl of the Pacific was now our warm and gracious home. It was the year she turned forty, a knockout by all rights—Mother was stunning. She effortlessly clung to her dancer's body; most of her five foot two inch frame was legs. The kind of women that hushes a room when she walks into it. Majestic Spanish beauty.

It was indisputably Mama's talent that revamped the nightclub, Tequila Le Club, creating a fabulous success. Her fame was not limited to the locals. It was the late '70s, and word of this over-the-top review made its way to international acclaim. Mia Farrow and Harold Robbins were just two of the many celebrities that La Mama had associated with because of the show. Rumors had been floating around town that Mr. Sammy Davis, Jr. was coming to see the performance one night. As Mama recalls that evening her emerald eyes light up with excitement:

"It was 9:30 p.m. when I realized that the DJ was not showing up for work...with no backup disc jockey available on such short notice, my only option was to do it myself."

Anyone else would have been mortified, but not La Mama—she thrived when faced with a challenge. She excelled under pressure.

"I knew my way around the sound booth because I had used it during rehearsals. To my disappointment there was not one Sammy Davis, Jr. album in the place, so I popped in a prerecorded cassette and made a mad dash for my apartment, a few blocks away. My effort paid off; later that same night Mr. Davis walked in. His infamous smile beamed with approval as he placed his hands on his waist and enjoyed my selection of music.

"'*The candy man can, as he mixes it with love and makes the world go round...*' He mouthed the words and snapped his fingers in time to his recent musical hit as he and his wife, Altovise, made their way to the table at the front of the stage.

From the DJ booth I watched with fascination Mr. Davis's reaction to each number in my show. Sitting deep in his chair, his legs stretched out, he rested his feet on the small raise of the stage. He cheered and applauded with the rest of the audience as he threw back another martini. After the show, back in the dressing room, the performers and I celebrated a job well done. The mood was intoxicating; we screamed and hugged, and there was such a commotion that we didn't even notice him walk in.

"'Hey, cats!' his unmistakable voice announced. 'Who's the choreographer? I wanna meet the choreographer!'

"'I have been such a huge fan of the whole Rat Pack,' I explained. As a teenager Frank Sinatra stole my heart, but Sammy was the dancer. Mr. Bojangles himself! His huge gold rings reflected in every direction as he extended his hand for mine.

"'That was great! I loved it!" Sammy hugged and kissed me, much to my delight; his wife nodded in acceptance."

That moment was frozen in time with a single flash from the house photographer. La Mama, the dancers in the show, Mr. Sammy Davis, Jr., and his lovely wife smiled for the camera.

Life was paradise.

A divine currant had taken us upstream. We were safe, happy, and well taken care of. Some twenty years later would eventually reveal how much danger we had actually averted.

3

DANCING UP A STORM

Four dancing daughters. Four young women. Well, teenagers technically—my baby sister Paula was just sixteen when she moved into my flat in the city; she had already been performing professionally since thirteen. A dance company that I auditioned for in Acapulco provided the talent for a weekly television variety show, *Siempre en Domingo* (Always on Sunday).We filmed all week from the Televisa station in Mexico City.

My sister Lisa, after many years banging out her zapateado as a folklore dancer at the blistering hot outdoor convention center in Acapulco, moved triumphantly onto Mexico City's Broadway stage, in the role of Morales in *A Chorus Line*. The eldest, Carmen, choose to stay at the convention center where she danced with the world famous Gauchos, from Argentina. We all traveled back and forth from Mexico City to Acapulco, dancing up a storm and consistently eluding wickedness and harm's way.

I always found that a wonderful sense of spirituality lived deep and untouched in my genuine core. Living in one of the most dangerous places in the world, a countless amount of times I was attacked, once with a knife, and almost raped. I began to realize that a divine power shielded me. Though no religion to guide me, I felt the need to dance for God, for my angels; I danced to say thank you for the many blessings bestowed upon me.

* * *

September 19, 1985
(excerpt from article)

The 1985 Mexico City earthquake was a magnitude 8.1 earthquake that struck Mexico on 19 September 1985 at 7:19 local time, causing the deaths of about 10,000 people and serious damage in the nation's capital.

To this day, the death toll has been in dispute. About 5,000 bodies were recovered from the debris and represent the total of legally certified deaths but does not include those who were missing and never recovered. Reports have numbered the dead anywhere from 5,000 to 30,000 (claimed by a number of citizens' groups) to 45,000 claimed by the Mexican National Seismological Centre. However, the death toll was great enough to necessitate the use of the IMSS baseball field as a morgue, using ice to conserve bodies for identification. This earthquake had significant long-term political consequences for the country.[1] The complete seismic event consisted of four quakes.

The energy released during the main event was equivalent to approximately as far away as Los Angeles and Houston.

* * *

Paula was traveling on the subway that ill-fated morning in September. She survived the earthquake by climbing out of a hole in the concrete and dodging the falling debris. I was miles away in Guadalajara with my young family, ripped with fear.

The television station, Televisa, where we had worked not too long ago, was completely destroyed. Everyone was killed. I was not surprised at all with Paula's decision to take my mother and move to Toronto, Canada, where they started a now very successful dance studio, opening doors and building bridges for myself, my children, and my sister Lisa, so that we could cross over gracefully into the Promised Land.

Just like a heavenly classical orchestral arrangement, I flew through the warm spring meadows of Toronto, listening to my childrens' laughter, a sweet gift from God. We boarded the island ferry for a day of fun and togetherness. We had traveled thousands of miles away from the ugliness of the explosion, into another world.

Looking across the cool blue waters of Lake Ontario, I took a deep breath. I knew that we were safe once again. Here, I could give them and myself a fresh start. This was going to be our new home, I decided. I was happy. I was free. I took a job teaching ballet, which I loved, and my children were adapting very nicely. *Raul will just have to realize at some given time that I'm not going back to him*, I thought. *He will be fine...*

Seest thou a man wise in his own conceit? There is more hope of a fool than of him.
—Proverbs 26:12

4

PREMONITION/PREVIOUS WARNING/HUNCH/SUSPICION

Suspect? I should have known. After almost ten years of marriage, I should have been most certain that Raul, with all of his "I was once famous" ego, was not going to let me get away that effortlessly. In Latin culture, like many cultures, the woman is forbidden to walk away from her home: *abandono del hogar* (abandonment of the home), a crime that I now stood guilty of.

Bright yellow daffodils in the dusk of April's light, the red-breasted robin appeared for the first time of the season; another winter was over. Signs of survival were constantly among us. Signs of demise could be also. Days turned into months, then almost a year, and still no retaliation from the husband I had run away from. The storm clouds were forming, though—powerful, dark, and angry. My gift of prophecy, my guardian angel, tried to forewarn me, clear as the Caribbean sea; I saw, in a dream, the events that would come to pass in the days to follow.

Late in October, on a cool autumn night, my heavy head hit the pillow, and somewhere between fear and imagination, I dreamed of Raul walking a long stretch of airport gates.

* * *

I recognize these gates; blue, red, I see Delta Airlines, American Airlines...I know this place, it's Dallas–Fort Worth. On and on he's walking, heels clicking on the cold tiles of the busy airport. He is strutting confidently though, in his signature cowboy boots, faded jeans, tweed sports jacket with the sleeves rolled up, outdated sunglasses, thick mustache, and long blond curly hair flowing like a shampoo commercial. He stops to talk to a ticket agent; she smiles at him graciously. As he speaks his tongue turns into a forked snake's tongue, whipping and slithering from side to side. He removes his glasses slowly and reveals his tiny vermin red eyes. The woman is unaware of his evil lies and gives him a boarding pass. Over his shoulder is a large black duffel bag, slightly unzipped. My eyes pan in like a zoom lens. The bag has a tiny brown ponytail exposed, clipped with a pink ballerina barrette—dear God! It's Tiffany!

* * *

I screamed with horror and my gasp slapped me out of my sleep.

That morning, I felt the shadow of my nightmare accompany me as I went about my daily routines. As I walked the kids to school I felt a lasting bitter taste in my mouth, like when you've been sick with the flu. My dream was so vivid, it haunted me for hours. Was it mother's intuition, or my inevitable payment for leaving him? Divine intervention? Or all of the above? The truth was no matter how confident I felt in my surroundings then, he would find a way to punish me sooner or later. So I took a deep breath and gave him a call. Maybe he would tell me that he was doing fine, that he'd meet someone new—anyway, for my own peace of mind, I had to face him.

I find a quiet spot in the house and make the phone call.

"Si bueno," Nora, his mother, answered.

"How are you, Señora?" I tried to hide my emotions from her. She seemed surprised by my call but didn't offer any well-wishes for me or the children.

"Raul, *she* is calling you!" Nora shouted through the house.

Moments later Raul took the phone, clearing his throat as he answered my call; I could feel him taking his time to speak, as if preparing himself for this conversation.

"I miss you," he said. "Are you missing me too?" He didn't even wait for a response from me. "Annamaria, I've decided to sell everything and move to Canada to be with you and the children." His lies are forming like white-tipped waves off the coastline.

Again he didn't wait for my response. Instead he continued to sell me his plan; like a fast-talking scenartist, he was over the top with urgency.

"That's great, when?" It was a good thing he couldn't see my face, the uncertainty in my eyes.

"Soon my love, it will happen very soon."

The absoluteness of his voice frightened me to death, but I didn't dare show it. With the excuse of the cost of the long-distance phone call I graciously cut him off with a quick goodbye, and a lie.

"I love you too."

What is going on? I wrestled with my thoughts for days after that call. *This could be a good thing.* I tried to convince myself to give him a second chance. My argument with myself was a good one. The children needed their father. Here it would be different. He had no control over me. I was just earning a modest dance teacher's salary. The style of life that I had become accustomed to had been downgraded immensely—perhaps with a little persuading I could at least get back a portion of my wealth. When I left Raul gained control over all of my investments, the house, the two taxis I bought, and the kids' college funds. Besides all that, he was not that bad...

* * *

For the love of money is the root of all evil: which while some coveted after, they have erred from the faith, and pierced themselves through with many sorrows.
—*1 Timothy 6:10*

* * *

On a quiet suburban cul-de-sac, my sister Lisa and I rented a spacious house next to a park, close to the school and fifteen minutes from the dance studio we both worked at. The neighborhood was lovely and very picturesque. The children were free to play on the swing sets into the early dusk and wander between houses to visit with all of their new friends. We took our children to dance with us and also took turns babysitting. Lisa, along with her husband Librado, and I had made a new life in this place.

Life's daily events grant a sense of false comfort. I put Raul out of my head for the moment. As days went by, my vivid nightmare faded like the morning dew, kissed by sweet warm sunlight.

Driving home from work that night Tiffany and Carlo were home waiting for me. I parked my car, unloaded some groceries, and walked in through the front door. Carlo was setting on the steps waiting for me. It was after nine o'clock and he was just five years old; he should have be in bed by then.

"Hey, baby, why are you still up?" The sound of my own

voice revealed my anxious demeanor. He looked up at me and I knew, I just instantly knew, something was wrong...

"Where is Tiffany, baby?" I was trying so hard not to show him my tension, fraught for his response.

"Daddy came and took her, we were playing on the swings and came and he took her to the mall, he said for me to go inside to get my toys and he would take me too, but when I came outside they were gone..." He looked so sad.

I tried not to panic but was completely unsuccessful. *Your Daddy? Your Daddy is here!*

"The mall? Are you sure, baby? Are you *sure* it was Daddy?" He nodded solemnly. "I'll be right back then." I heard my own voice tremble. "They need a ride back, I'm just going to find them. You go on up to bed and I'll see you when I get home." I tried to reassure him, gave a kiss and a little smile while my heart frantically raced.

That moment, that fleeting moment, hit me with the horror of a runaway train. I took off out the door, no shoes, no coat, keys in hand. I started the car and raced to Hillcrest Mall, all the while calculating hours in my mind. *I left for work at 3:30 pm, it's now 9:45 pm; that's six hours...* I pulled up to the mall and leapt out of the car, leaving the door open and the engine running. The haunting wide hallways of the mall echoed as I ran barefoot down each one screaming her name.

"Excuse me Miss!" The security guard stopped me. "This mall has been closed for almost an hour now," he said politely. "No one is here, not that I've seen." He gave a reassuring eye contact.

I knew that he spoke the truth, no one was there...it was a lie. Trembling and mortified, I raced back home again. This time Lisa was waiting by the door.

"I've called the police." She bit her lip as she spoke. "He can't get far," she affirmed with certainty.

"It wasn't Raul!" Librado her husband shouted as he walked towards us, arms waving with anger. "Raul would have come in for a drink, to say hello. He's Mexican, he's family." Librado seemed very sure of his judgment.

My head felt light and my vision began to fade. *I'm going to pass out.*

The doorbell rang and the phone shrilled at the same time, almost as if to say, "Are you going down for the count or are you stronger than him?" I answered the phone and Lisa got the door, thanking the police for coming so quickly.

On the phone, my mother delivered her findings, completely composed like a newscaster, deliberately and confidently. "She boarded a plane at 6:30 pm to Dallas." La Mama had already jumped into action; she continued to speak, but the words faded into the dark as I was thrown into my very own actual nightmare. I dropped the phone as tears of hysteria engulfed me and I fell back, like an egg hurled against a wall, smashing on impact and slowly pulled down by gravity. It was real, he had taken her, she was gone.

"Annamaria, my name is Detective Sergeant Ground, and this is my partner, Detective Dennis Le Plant." They nodded at me, looking for a response.

I tried to converge my thoughts; one, no two, large police officers stood over me. They squatted down beside me and began to speak.

"We understand that there has been an abduction by your estranged husband. Are you positive he has the child?" They spoke slowly and waited patiently for answers. I heard myself speaking, somehow; I tapped into reserves, gained composure, and I carefully explained, to the best of my knowledge, the information that my mother had made herself privy to.

The phone rang again.

"Annamaria?" La Mama was clearly more concerned.

"Yeah, Mom." Now I was holding on to her every word like a lifesaver gone overboard.

"Now listen...they made it to Dallas, but there isn't a flight out of Dallas to Mexico until noon tomorrow. You can be on the 9:30 am flight and catch up to them before they get on their next flight. Honey, listen...you have to stop them before they get back into Mexico." She gave pause.

"Annamaria?" Mama waited for me to answer.

"Si Mama." I'd stopped crying.

"I don't have to tell you how hard its going to be if they cross that border." She said, "I'll make arrangements to have the Dallas police meet you at the airport. I'm booking your flight right now."

"Gracias Mama," I stammered.

* * *

Dark October night fell like a sleeping lion, powerful and still. I held vigil by my window. I couldn't even try to rest, not with my little girl out there. To close my eyes would be to give in to the situation, to succumb, subside, surrender. So I sat by the glass and gazed down at the very swing sets where she played some hours ago, lit by the great harvest moon, blowing in the wind with perfect rhythm, hauntingly, as if she still was down there. My heart quivered and the tears showed no sign of cessation.

The blue moonlight began to flood my room. I imagined it to be actual ocean water; the torrent of icy current crashes against the four walls of my room. Instinctively, my chest felt heavy and I felt myself drowning.

"Oh God help me, Please dear God, only You can help me. I can't breathe, I can't take the pain," I prayed without restraint.

"*Just breathe,*" through the wind came angelic whispers. I complied and the mythical flood retreated.

Peace I leave with you, my peace I give unto you: not as the world giveth, give I unto you. Let not your heart be troubled, neither let it be afraid.
 —*John 14:27*

5

SEEK AND YE SHALL FIND

"Humans need to go through a certain amount of change before they're ready for spirituality."
—*Echart Toll*

Dawn broke on that quiet suburb without hesitation, without pride or prejudice for the storm that had past through the day before. The light on the tiny houses seemed supernatural and askew, and the air felt thick and cold. I emerged from that night with a new skin. I felt something inside of me had changed; I felt enormous, sharpened, accelerated, and yes, angry. I knew that I must chase and face Raul and get my daughter back. Armed with legal documents and flight itineraries, I must first take pause from army mode to Mother mode and try to explain to my baby boy, that I, too, must leave.

"Carlito." I kissed his tiny face and tried to wake him.

"Mummy, did you find Tiff?" His question caused a lump in my throat.

"Not yet, baby." I was doing my very best not to cry. I continued to explain. "I have to go to another city to get her. I should be back home in a day or two." As I spoke the words seemed too outrageous to be true, and the grandeur of my task was unveiling in front of me.

His beautiful hazel eyes filled to the brim with tears. "Does this mean I have to have breakfast without Tiffany again?" He bit down on his lip and I could see the stress that this situation was causing him.

I gave him a long warm hug, wiped the tears from his cheeks, and assured him that she would be back home in no time. Setting aside the time restraint of my travels, I brushed the hair from his face and sang quietly to him. His eyes held onto mine as he drifted into slumber; I murmured, "I'll get her back. I promise."

Capturing his pain like a Venus fly trap, I need it to grow, to power me on my mission.

I will end this now, today. I will ambush him and I will get my daughter back.

It was still very early in the morning, and while the rest of the world went about their daily life, the business-class travelers planned the day's meetings. I planned my assault.

* * *

The plane touched down in the middle of the pouring rain; even though I was on foreign soil, the authorities were more than accommodating. They greeted me with that famed southern hospitality and instantly I felt empowered with allies. After a quick meeting and after they examined my documentation, we took a very long walk over to gate 32B. Delta Airlines, American Airlines...disturbingly, I realized I was walking down the same blue and red hallways that Raul walked in my dream earlier that week. The thought was both haunting and sobering. It was not a dream, I was living it.

Flight 185 to Guadalajara would be boarding in less than an hour. Raul could be walking around the corner any minute with Tiffany! The thought that I actually beat them to the plane made me sing and rejoice. I stood there, with a visible smug look. Larger than life.

Yeah, you think you're so smart, Raul. La Mama tapped into your plan too fast and now I got you!

I stood there just imagining the look on his face...when he walked around the corner...one day and one thousand miles later, only to be busted! Ha! I shook my shoulders and shivered for a second, savoring in vain the moment. That moment turned into an hour or so as I impatiently watched the entire flight board. One by one I studed the faces with intensity as they filed in front of me, on their way to Guadalajara.

The door shut and I tenaciously refused to give up my ace. They were there, somewhere; I could feel it.

So, armed with the itinerary of all of the upcoming flights to anywhere in Mexico, I bid goodbye to the officers that sympathetically stood by my side and headed to the next terminal with the same furor that I arrived with.

Calmly, I justified my every thought. *Of course Raul would not take a direct flight to Guadalajara; he is too smart for that.* I opened my list of upcoming flights and decided which was my smartest strategy, a typical desperate gambler at the race track. Each name spoke out to me...

Mexico City! He has family there.

So once again I stood at another gate and watched as the passengers board. Like a poker player that loses yet another hand, the door shut on a third, fourth, and fifth flight...I refused to believe that I'd lost. Until all of my chips were swept away from me...

By now the whole airport was alerted, and I didn't have to physically run from gate to gate; I was told that if they were in the Dallas–Fortworth airport security would notify me. I just could not trust; I had to be there myself at every gate. Too much was at stake. How could I rely on these strangers with such a monumental task? Mama told me my child, my baby, was there. Contradicting my flurry of hysteria for time were airport clocks that marked the constant reminder that the window of opportunity had long shut in a loud slam.

The last flight had boarded.

Nine hours of running, of justifying, of hoping and believing, swept away. As the last door closed, the airline attendant gave me a somber look. Right to the bitter end, with reluctant anguish and distress, I headed to a modest hotel room with deep sigh of defeat, kicked off my shoes, and crawled into bed.

In a effort to drown out the sound of planes taking off, and my insane thoughts of her on every one of them, I turned on the TV.

The broadcaster's voice filled the room.

"Tonight on NBC, Sally Field stars in a the chilling true drama, *Not Without My Daughter*."

Horrified, I watched in awe. Sally Field's character was desperately searching for her daughter, who had been kidnapped by her estranged husband and taken to Iran. Was it art imitating life? Or was it just sinister people using their kids to gain control over their spouses—or worse, vengeance? My mind wandered away from the film as I tried to imagine how I was going to get my *own* daughter back in my arms. My task was enormous, just like my will...but narcissism was transformed into modesty.

Faith was bestowed upon me. I found myself deep in anguished prayer for divine intervention.

Although I didn't find Tiffany on that trip, I did find a side of me that I always knew existed—an inner strength, a spiritual fountain of optimism, which I could no longer deny or abandon, for my childrens' sake as well as my own.

Ask, and it shall be given you; seek and ye shall find. Knock and it shall be opened unto you.
—*Matthew 7:7–8*

6

THE DEMONS OF DOUBT

Twilight was upon our neighborhood as I pulled up in my airport taxi. The jack-o'-lanterns began to flicker in the thick cold air. All Hallows' Eve had arrived, and with it the demons of my very own hell. I entered the house without fanfare or victory; the trial of my journey had accosted me. Still, I tried to put up a good front for my baby boy. Thankfully he was dressing for trick-or-treats; excitedly he ran into my arms.

"Mama!" Carlito wrapped his arms around my neck tightly.

"Hey baby, what are you doing sweetie?" Just being around him gave me back a reason to live.

"Auntie Lisa made us costumes for tonight! Come see, Mommy, come see!" He was just so excited to show me, it took him a few minutes to realize that I didn't bring Tiffany home.

"Mama, where is Tiff?" The question crackled as it left his innocent mouth.

"I didn't find her yet...but I will soon." I whispered, perhaps because the words hurt terribly. I needed to give him back his moment of joy again, so I asked to see his costume.

"What are those?" I laughed honestly at the large white and black painted boxes on the basement floor.

"They're dice!" he said proudly. "Lisa made them for me and Tiffany," he explained.

"Tiff is going to miss Halloween," he said sadly. "I miss her too much, Mommy." He sat down, and I sat down on the floor with him.

We both stared at the dice costumes for awhile in silence.

"Mommy, what's dice called when its only one?" He reflected deeply on the moment.

I answered him so quickly my words left my mouth without my permission.

"Its called a die," I say with a lump in my throat.

"Oh...die," he repeated.

The doorbells chimed along with a strong authoritative knock, rudely interrupting our sad moment. I gave Carlito a kiss and hurried up the stairs. At the door, the same two officers, Detective Le Plant and his partner, Sergeant Ground, visited my unrested home again. We spoke briefly of my unsuccessful voyage to the Dallas airport and I noticed them making eye contact as if, by my defeat, I had confirmed a hunch that they might have.

"We spoke to your sister-in-law, Leticia." Detective Le Plant delivered the update.

"She says your ex-husband doesn't have your daughter." His demeanor was sincere. His words were horrific.

"She is a wicked liar!" I lashed out in disbelief.

"Annamaria, we know that this is very difficult for you but we need to talk calmly and put our heads together so we can find Tiffany." He nodded reassuringly. "Where did your mother get that information about the flight to Dallas?" his partner questioned me; while taking his notes he added, "We have no confirmation that they were on that flight."

"She made some calls when it first happened...my mother said they boarded that flight to Dallas...Carlo said he saw him! Raul took Tiffany! Of course he took her—who else could have taken her? *Who else could have taken her?* Who has my little girl? Who..." My voice gave into a sobering cry as

THE DEMONS OF DOUBT

I relived the past few days and the anguish of the possibility.

I was completely frustrated, overwhelmed, and defeated. The visit from the police that evening cast the ugliest of scenarios on my quickly thinning hope. I burst out of the house to gather my thoughts, walking the dark streets with the ghouls and goblins. Halloween, night of horror, night of ungodly spirits and sin. I hear their laughter in the wind; like flickering flames they dance around me, mocking my Lord. *Where is your God now? Where is your precious child?* They taunt me.

What good is a god that lets this happen? The spirits cackle and disappear into the night.

* * *

The next morning I awoke lethargic; my strength had vanished with the voices in the night. Still I was haunted by the demons of doubt. Where *is* my baby? If *Raul* didn't take her…my head spun and I fought the very breath that murmured the question, as if it were my archnemesis. Disgusted with my newfound helplessness, I was conquered and powerless from the grip of dark evils of doubt.

In the hallway I could hear the sound of little feet running toward my door. A wave of heat rose up through my body as if a someone had thrown a switch and I realized I still had one child who needed me to hold it together and wake up from my self-pity.

We walked a few blocks to school that day with sun in our eyes. Carlito was only six years old, but he knew that something was terribly wrong. I remained cautious with my questioning as not to upset him. But the truth is, he saw her last. My son assured me that he saw Tiffany leave with Raul. I tried to find optimism in his words, but my doubt reminded me that he was just a child, and had not seen his father in almost a year. I took a deep breath and held him very close to say goodbye as I walked him into the lobby of the school. He kissed me and I felt so thankful that I was not looking for *both* of them. I watched him walk into his classroom until I could see that he was getting uncomfortable that I was still standing there and all of the other parents had gone.

As I turned to toward the main door to exit, I noticed some of the students' artwork was on display. One piece in particular caught my attention, so I moved towards it for a closer look. It was a pair of ballet shoes, done in paper mache, pink and lightly dusted with glitter. They gave off an air of fantasy and magic. "That's fabulous," I said out loud, and I felt a tiny bit grateful for the joy of that piece, so I moved in closer to acknowledge the artist name.

It read, *Tiffany Briseno, grade three.*

Dear God! With every ounce of power that it took to get out of bed that morning I stood there in the lobby of the school just crying silently, physically frozen by my pain. Unable to collect myself, I felt the teachers come to get me. They gently moved me into the office and spoke quietly amongst themselves. I saw my reflection in their eyes, the expressions on their faces, the perturbation. I was a ghastly shadow of who I was just days ago.

"What shall we tell the other children?" Mrs. Levine whispered.

The room stayed silent; no one answered her.

We stood in a circle, the teachers, the principals, the secretaries, the mothers...the women of the village. We stood in a circle weaving an imaginary quilt of comfort...some with their heads bowed down, scouring the floor for answers, others, their heads titled up, fighting back the tears. We stood in a circle because that's what women do—we comfort each other when things go wrong, with family, with husbands,

THE DEMONS OF DOUBT

with children...there is great comfort in numbers. We stood in silence; no one offered up advice or suggested vengeance... we stood weaving our imaginary quilt, just like the women of days of yore...

The principal drove me home, where the sympathetic ladies from Child Find had been waiting for me. All the questions repeatedly circled my mind like sharks on their path to attack. Still, I realized that this was a vessel that, ultimately, could bring her home, could end the pain. So I did my very best to accommodate them, and in return they assured me that everyone was looking for Tiffany. Everyone, everywhere.

That night after work I returned to Tiffany's room. I sat on her bed and admired her belongings. It made me feel close to her, or perhaps I was looking for a sign of sorts, a clue to her disappearance, her abduction. Did she know she was leaving? Would she not have taken something...anything? I walked around, doing a visual inventory of her room. Dance competition trophies adorned the shelves, carefully placed ribbons and gold metals hang from each one. Highest Overall Score, one reads; Junior Soloist, reads another...is she a soloist now? Did she run away?

My sight was blurred with tears as I tried to remember the last time that I saw her...

* * *

"Look Mommy, isn't it beautiful?" Her big brown eyes light up with excitement. "I made this in school today, It's for you...it's beautiful, right Mommy?" "Not as beautiful as you, Princess. Try and sleep now, its getting late. Te quiero hija. I love you, baby."

* * *

I found myself talking to her picture.

I continued praising her fabulous sense of style and design as if she were right there in the room showing me her accomplishments. On the window ledge I noticed an ceremonial statue of an angel that I'd never seen before. *Angel de la guarda,* the guardian angel. I made a mental note to ask my sister Lisa if she gave that religious relic to my daughter; it looked Mexican. I picked up the angel and walked back to my room, holding it across my chest like a cadaver ready for burial. I slowly melted down over the covers of my bed and stared out the window at the night sky.

There is a possibility that a stranger may have taken your daughter.

As my eyes closed, my head spun.

The oversized glass of pinot noir was numbing the pain in my body but not my mind; my thoughts haunted me in the silence of night. *What could I have done to stop him? Does Mama know? Why didn't I listen to my premonition? How did I not see this coming...was it Raul...or someone else?* The magnet of exhaustion pulls into a deep slumber and in an instant I am standing in front of a paper wall...a white paper wall.

* * *

A small rip allows light and an eerie fog to seep in. I tear a larger hole in the wall with my bare hands and step through. The ground is cruel and steely and I walk barefoot; it is painful but I feel compelled to continue. In my travels I encounter a forest of sorts. The trees all have faces, unfamiliar faces, strangers. They move into a line and begin to question me. Where is your second child? They speak in turns, with authority, like a grand council. The trees are dressed in religious robes and have giant crucifixes hanging from their necks. I am angry and frightened by them but I dare not show it, so I shout back my response. "He's home in bed!" I answer.

"Nooooo! Your second child is the girl!" He retorts.

"We know you had an abortion, you killed your first child. God doesn't like murderers. Perhaps God took your child...an eye for an eye!" They snicker at their justice. "Murderer," they chant.

"That's a LIE!" I scream. "God loves me, he loves my children. God gives, he does not take away! The devil takes, you are devils, all of you! Damn you!" I kick and punch them, trying in vain to break their branches. A battle ensues and they begin throwing rocks and fireballs at me. I try to dart, but one hits me on my right side. I fight to extinguish the flames. Hundreds of trees shuffle together to keep me from escaping the forest. I manage to squeeze by them and dash into the clear. There I discover a dimly lit spot where someone had incautiously buried something. A pale pink box, a large toy chest. I see a corner of the chest revealed, white satin ballet slippers embellished on one side. Frantically I run over to it and begin digging at it with my bare hands. I brush the icy soil from the chest like an accomplished archeologist trying to preserve his find. Inside I discover a young child's arms sliced at the elbows, her torso still dressed in a tutu, her innocent head, carefully placed on top of the other body parts...it's Tiffany...

I scream, and my scream throws me back into reality...

* * *

Gasping and crying, I awoke from my nightmare. Bewildered and spooked, I jumped out of bed. I looked down at my feet as they hit the carpet. They were covered in cold soil; my hands were scraped and dirty and my pant legs were wet from the snow. Mortified, I realized that I must have been outside in the park next door. I brought home tormenting souvenirs of my voyage into a mother's unimaginable horror. I stumbled into my bathroom. Still breathless from my dream, I washed the dirt from my hands and feet. I felt pain on my side and lifted my shirt to investigate its source. A bright red spot marked the place where the fireball hit me in my nightmare! "What the...devil?" Dazed and confused, I tried splashing cold water on my face. In the mirror the stream of relentless tears cascaded in silence.

I made my way over to Carlo's room, and without waking him I lifted his tiny body and took him back to my bed. Curling myself around him I listened to rhythm of his breathing. It soothed me like a mother's zen-ful lullaby. I pushed my face into his hair and felt the heat coming off his precious head.

As I gently gazed out the center of my window, a single star's light caught my attention. As it twinkled in the heavens, I heard a voice, faint but clear. *She's all right child, don't lose your faith...just hold on...grow...* The voice filled my room like a night light, scaring away the monsters that I created. I was left with a feeling of quietude, a quiet stillness. I must have faith, I needed to believe. Because the magnitude of my search needs not only included the globe, but the heavens themselves...she can't be dead...she's alive.

Some clouds drifted across the night sky and covered the little star's light, yet somehow the light stayed in my room. I drifted with the clouds floating across the virtuous sky, searching; an entire army of celestial angels joined me, and became my closest allies. Somewhere between imagination and reality, conscious and subconscious, the voice whispered again, *Voluntad de Dios, God's Will, you will find her*. I heard

THE DEMONS OF DOUBT

a church choir singing from every corner of the worshipping world, *Our Father who art in heaven, Hollowed be thy Name...*

I sought the Lord, and he heard me, and delivered me from all my fears. They looked unto him, and were lightened: and their faces were not ashamed.
—Psalm 34:4, 5

7

RESCUE ME

At the kitchen table, that morning, Carlito sat having his breakfast. That morning he had set two places, one for himself and one for Tiffany. I overheard him in full conversation with her, in his mind.

"That's funny, Tiff!" he laughed.

"No, I didn't do it," he answered.

I watched him go through his dialogue with a sick taste in my mouth. I'd been so busy looking for Tiffany that I had neglected her brother's emotions. I felt guilt-stricken.

"Good morning Mommy," he said cheerfully as he turned and looked at me.

"Tiff doesn't want me to tell you," he said sheepishly.

"Tell me what?" I'm afraid of the answer.

"She did a fart!" he laughed.

"Yes you did!" He enjoyed antagonizing his imaginary sister.

"She did?" I replied, unsure of his behavior.

He got down from his chair at the table and walked over to me. "Mommy, my chest hurts when I breath like this." He held his heart and mine melted.

"Well, lets go see Dr. Dave and see if he can fix it. Okay?" I tried not to let my voice crack. With one child missing, if the other should fall ill, I would surely have lost what was left of my sanity.

Later that day during Carlos's weekly soccer practice he collapsed on the field and the paramedics took him to Sick Kids Hospital.

The doctor explained that Carlito was experiencing asthma due to stress, which cut off his oxygen, causing him to collapses. He gave him medication and asked me how a six-year-old can be under so much stress.

"He is very close to his sister, who..." It took me a minute to say the words. "Has been missing for almost a month now." I looked down in shame.

"May I suggest that he speak with someone?" the doctor said quietly.

"My son is not crazy. He just misses his sister terribly," I retorted.

"Still, if he is this upset...it wouldn't hurt to have some help for him," he insisted. "What about yourself? How are you coping with all of this?" The doctor took a deeper analyzing look at me.

"My child is missing and the other is sick with grief. How am I doing?" I said sadly. My thoughts turned to the previous night's nightmare.

I paused with hesitation.

"What do you think did this?" The doctor looked confused that I had changed the conversation so quickly. I lifted my shirt and showed him the mark on my side where the fireball had hit me in my dream.

"It looks like frostburn," he said. "Were you outside for any long periods of time without a jacket?" He sounded concerned.

I darted my eyes around the examination room, looking for an answer that wouldn't sound insane.

"I...I don't know," I said honestly.

I took my baby boy home and tucked him into bed, silently vowing to end his pain...soon.

I watched helplessly as he withered like a freshly cut flower deprived of water. Each morning at breakfast he would ask for Tiffany.

"I think it should be this week," I would say repeatedly.

But weeks turned into months, and just when all avenues had been exhausted, Christmas came, and with it, a tiny miracle—a word from God via a little Jewish girl named Sasha. Finally a ray of hope shined on a cold winter's day.

I was teaching my ballet class that day, a class that was especially difficult because that was Tiffany's favorite. She had made a very close friend, like little girls do; Sasha and Tiff were inseparable. Sasha came to me after class.

"Um, Anna, I have to tell you something." She looked around like she had a secret.

I was not ready for what she was about to say. The truth is I didn't even think to ask her if she knew something about Tiffany; I just assumed that she was just as surprised as everyone else when she went missing.

"I was at shoal on Saturday...and something that the Rabbi said told me that I have to tell the truth," she continued. "Tiff told me not to tell you but I have to tell the truth. God wants me to tell you." The nine-year-old looked me in the eyes as if she knew the severity of her words.

"Tiff knew that she was going back to Mexico with her dad...she said that she had to do it to save her parents' marriage...if she went back to Mexico with her Daddy you would have to follow them." Sasha twisted up her mouth; she felt good, a burden was lifted. Her Rabbi was right: the truth was a good thing.

I was not angry at that child for hiding that precious best friend's secret. Relieved—that was the third testimony supporting the idea that Raul, not a stranger, had taken Tiffany. It made perfect sense. But why then had he not contacted me to say that he had her? If I ever wanted to see my daughter again I would run back to him, back to the place where he was in control. His domain. Mexico.

La Mama was not surprised at the revelation. I watched her calculably pick up her phone and summon an international lawyer that she had waiting in the wings. I listened attentively as they spoke of the Hague Convention, an international agreement that enables a government to ask the host country to ensure that a child is returned to their place of abduction until a judge can determine custody. Mexico had just signed that treaty. Still, we had to locate her. The Attorney General also had a new program called simply Project Return, paired with Child Find and the strength of the great RCMP. It appeared that all of the Canadian authorities had teamed in my favor, which would have been spectacular, if she was in Canada. Mexico had its challenges; corruption was a big one.

Mama spent many days working with the authorities to get her granddaughter back; she always had faith in the system. She was, as long as I could remember, not a person of faith in the Lord. She was a good person. With strong values, not a religious person, she had no church home to call her own.

Mama called a family meeting at her condo one afternoon to discuss our plans to find Tiffany in Mexico.

There was a lull in the conversation when I realized that I had not seen Carlo in a while.

"Where is Carlo?" I turned to my sister Lisa as soon as I discovered that I had not seen him leave the condo.

"He went outside to play," she said calmly.

I walked over to the window and looked down at the creek that backed onto the property. The winter had been unusually warm and a lot of the rivers were starting to swell. Through the bare January trees I could see a blue ski jacket and I recognized it immediately.

It's Carlo and he is in the creek! Waist high!

* * *

In a millisecond I bolted for the door, not taking the time to explain my actions. Flying down the staircase, my cry echoed up the well.

No, no...Please, dear God...no...no...noooooo...

I shot out the back door and careened through the ravine. I burst into the icy torrent river, wading earnestly toward my son. Adrenaline in full throttle, I managed to pull him and myself from certain peril.

Sweet Jesus.

Back at the house I asked him why.

"I just don't want to feel the pain anymore," he confessed. "My feet felt numb and I was thinking that if I went in deeper I would feel numbing everywhere, all over it hurts, Mommy..." He cried, and I cried with him.

"But you know that Mommy loves you and that would be a very bad thing, right?" I tried to explain.

"Yes Mama," He answered.

"It's a good thing I didn't go with Daddy too, right?" he said.

"It's a very good thing, baby!" I smiled honestly.

"Why didn't Daddy take me too?" he asked.

I wasn't ready for the question. It had been months since she had been gone. Everyone had asked me that same question, everyone except the only one that had a real right to know.

"Only God knows, baby," I answered. "But I tell you this, sure as the sun shines each morning...I will find Tiffany and I will bring her home!" My words had a true conviction that I had never spoke before and my son knew it.

"I promise you, but you have to promise that you won't do anything like what you did today while I'm gone." I looked

deep into his hazel eyes; I needed to see that he understood.
"Pinkie swear," he said.
"Pinkie swear," I repeated.

8

ALL THE KING'S HORSES AND ALL THE KING'S MEN...

Guadalajara, Mexico's second largest city. This Spanish Colonial masterpiece is home to over eight million inhabitants. The Centro Historico is the most charming part of downtown with its pedestrian-only streets, intricate fountains, and buildings dating back to the early 1500s.

Guadalajara is not only a center of mariachi music, but also a stronghold of *charreadas* (the Mexican version of the rodeo) and the popular folk dance, the *Jarabe Tapatío*—three things which to the foreigner express the very essence of Mexican folk traditions. One notable event in the history of the town includes Miguel Hidalgo's declaration of the abolition of slavery in 1810. The central feature of Guadalajara is a magnificent group of four squares, arranged in the form of a cross, with the city's principle public buildings set around them.

La Mama and I flew into the valley of Atemajac, less than a week after Sasha divulged her secret. Guadalajara showed no signs of the explosion that rocked the city's core in April of 1992. Later that day, we met with *judiciales*, local police, lawyers, and a judge. My mother had a lot of influential friends that she had made along the way. At one time in her life she was the personal fitness trainer to the former president of Mexico Miguel Allende's wife. Both my Mother and my older sister Carmen had a good friend that they referred to only as "the General."

Carmen flew up from Acapulco to help us find Tiffany. As the days passed and we searched unsuccessfully, I realized how little I knew about the man that I had been married to for almost ten years. It was a sobering thought. Had I been so consumed with myself, my career, my very image, that I had no room for anything else in my life? I didn't know his friends, where he hung out; I barely could recall where most of his eight brothers and sisters lived. At a stoplight I looked up and saw a billboard with a shoe advertisement that I was in. My face looked down on the city streets.

"You're still beautiful." My mother noticed me staring at my old billboard ad.

In the image above us, her eyes looked dead; there was no sparkle, no joy in her life. Even though I had it all.

That miserable time in Guadalajara, land of the faithful, surrounded by cathedrals, churches, and crosses, made me question the true grandeur of my own beliefs. There we were asking for help from all of these powerful people and I had not taken the time to pray to the Most Powerful of All. It was time to shed the old skin and reinvent myself. Time to grow, do some internal housecleaning.

Reset.

Rid myself of my destructive selfish ego, my worldly accomplishments, and focus on my spiritual existence.

Soul searching, getting closer to my Creator.

I had to truly believe that the only way that I was going to find my daughter and rescue my son was with His Divine Intervention...

* * *

On the flight back to Toronto, Mama assured me that we had made successful achievements in the search for Tiffany. She sat confidently, knowing that all of her people were looking for her granddaughter. The flight was completely booked, but Mother had ambitiously bought a seat for Tiffany that she did not cancel before we left. I saw her look over at the empty seat and turn away quickly so that I could not see her crying. As we flew over the majestic Sierra Madre, the people that she spoke of earlier seemed minuscule in comparison to those mountains that separated me and my child.

They that wait upon the Lord shall renew their strength, they shall mount up with wings of eagles.
—Isaiah 40:31

9

CONFRONTATION

Salvador was a good friend of mine, a proud Jewish Mexican from a prominent family that lived in Beverly Hills, California. Tall, slim, with a distinct nose that completely suited his bold persona, Salvador had a manufacturing plant in Guadalajara and was there on business when he learned of my situation. It was late in April; almost four months had passed since we found out that Raul had taken Tiffany and gone into hiding in Mexico. Salvador called me that morning, with the answer to my prayers.

"I have some news for you." He always sounded very businesslike, even when he spoke of matters of the heart.

"I heard of your predicament, so I had my people look for that no-good husband of yours..." I was hoping that he would get straight to the news but he was savoring his find, so I waited with the patience of a saint.

"We found him today. He is in a house in the Reforma section of town," he continued, even though he heard me asking repeatedly, "Where?"

"Thank you, Salvador, you're a godsend!" I proclaimed.

"I'm preparing for the raid with my judicials. I think that you should be here when it happens...your little girl has been through so much already, it would not be good for her to have to go into the children's aid until you come to get her." He had already claimed victory.

"I'll book my ticket as soon as I get off the phone with you," I affirmed.

"No need, you're already on the 6:30 flight to Dallas." He laughed.

"I will see you in the morning, my dear. We'll talk then, adios." Salvador hung up before I had a chance to thank him for his efforts; he was like that.

In the ten or so years that we had been friends he always searched for rewardless ways of helping people. He called it a *mitzvah*, an act of kindness that you would not necessarily benefit from. It was the way he lived his life. He loved his family, his children, and his God.

A 6:30 flight, the same one that they left on more than six months ago. Ironic, perhaps, but this time was different. This time I didn't have a fanfare for my victory.

The last six months had changed me forever. The pain and the prayer had crushed the block of black coal that I once was and a metamorphosis had occurred. Now I could listen to my angels. Now I was ready to hear my God.

I was ready for His promise, but before I left, there was a brave little soldier that needed to be assured that this time I would come home with his sister.

His eyes filled with tears when I told him that I was leaving yet again, a third time. He ran away from me as I tried to explain that this time was dissimilar. In a moment Carlo returned with the angelic Mexican statue, *angel de la guarda*, that I found in Tiffany's room.

"Take this with you, Mommy." He placed the angel in my hands carefully. "She will help you find Tiff," He explained.

"That's a great idea, thank you." I took the precious statue and carefully placed it in my purse. I kneeled down to give a hug. I raised my right hand to his forehead and motioned across with the words *Padre, Hijo, Espiritu Santo,* finished with a kiss on his head.

"She *will* help me find what I'm looking for...don't you forget to say your prayers too, I'm going to need them." My words lit his face.

"I'm going to pray sooo hard, Mommy, God will hear me this time!" He announced.

"He already does," gently I affirmed.

* * *

Jesus said "Let the children come to Me and do not hinder them, for the Kingdom of heaven belongs to such as these."
—Matthew 19:14

* * *

"Folks, we are now flying over the Sierra Madre, the southern extension of the great Cordillera system of North America...this mountain range extends more than 1100km, from the U.S. border all the way down the western coast of Mexico to our destination, Guadalajara. Its highest peak, just over 11,500 ft. If you can look over to the left side of the aircraft you may see a barranca, or canyon; that one exceeds 3300 feet in depth and rivals the Grand Canyon magnitude... without the tourists..." Our pilot let out a chuckle.

I was not amused. The magnitude of those mountains reminded me of the grandeur of my task.

God can move mountains...this time he is going to have to...

I knew that this time I could not fail. I must remain focused. Raul was down there...I looked out the window at the Sierra Madre, and Tiffany was with him. I would find them.

God as my witness.

"If you believe it...you can achieve it..." I repeated to myself. My heart pounded anxiously through my chest.

The taxi dropped me off very late that same night at the Federal Police station. *Federales*, they called them. An unethical terrorizing bunch, they do the devious work in Mexico, and true to stereotypes, they can be underhanded.

I spent the entire night at the station, coffee in hand, listening, watching, tirelessly waiting for our departure.

We climbed into a small fleet of tinted-windowed black SUVs and headed to our confrontation, fully armed and prepared for retaliation. I asked if the weapons were necessary—it was a custody affair, not a drug raid! I was told that the Federales are often encountered with gunfire. I felt as if we were putting my daughter at risk and I bowed my head to pray.

We swooped down over a modest house just before the dawn broke. My heart was racing with anticipation. The Federales knocked boldly on the front door and shouted, *"Policia abre la puerta!"*—Open the door!

After a moment they broke the handle right off and let themselves in. I motioned to exit the van but I was immediately stopped by the driver.

"No, Señora." He held my arm.

"But my daughter is in there!" I began to cry.

He let me out. Moments later the Federales came back out via the front door with angry demeanors.

"No one is in there," the chief said to me. "They must have known that we were coming," he explained.

"How is that possible?" I asked frantically.

"All is possible," he said cynically.

They motioned for me to get back in the car but I refused. I told them that I wanted to walk for a while and that I would be back at the station later. They pulled away in perfect unison like a choreographed scenario that they'd done a million times before.

I was disappointed but not surprised. I stood there staring at the house where Raul hid Tiffany.

This is where he was. Right here.

Even though we did not catch him, I silently thanked God for the moment...

The sunlight began to bleed over the roof tops and onto the lawn. The blessed light was caught by a twinkling sequin on a misplaced object concealed by the shrubbery. I walked over to it and cautiously pulled it from its hiding place. It was a ballerina bunny doll that I gave Tiffany last Easter! She was here! She is Alive! "God is good," I said aloud and kissed the toy as if I were kissing my child.

I walked down the busy morning streets of that neighborhood with the doll in my hand and a smile on my face. My energy and spirit were renewed. I knew that I was close, I could just feel it. Now more than ever, I had to put my faith in my Lord. I prayed again.

The supplicate bells of nearby church echoed from the north...just as I was about to turn in the opposite direction, I followed the chimes of the bells as if they were vocalizing my name.

They lead me to a modest local church, adjacent to a bustling marketplace. I stood in the doorway and contemplated entering.

"...we would ask you to please not attend our sanctuary again," the letter read. "I'm being kicked out of the church!" I laughed. *"You told them about my past?"* I shouted at Raul.

"You had an abortion, you know how they feel about that," he explained.

"That's no one's business!" I retaliated.

"My God is a forgiving God," I murmured to myself and walked righteously through the front door of the sanctuary. I kneeled and began to lay down my heavy burden.

"She is getting tall; it must be this desert air." A pure virtuous voice interrupted my prayers.

I looked up from where I knelt.

"You...saw her?" I was so enthralled with emotion that I struggled to speak.

"I see everything," He said, and a gentle smile broke across His face. He continued to speak.

"Go down to Lindavista Street...the house with no garden is where you will find your flower." I reached for His hand in gratitude, but He vanished right before my very eyes.

"Thank you Jesus! No one will ever believe me," I whispered.

"It doesn't matter really...I believe it." I sighed. I made the benediction on myself and exited the sanctuary with a respectful curtsy. Full of joy and excitement, I leaped down the staircase like a prima ballerina in full *jete*, arms above my head, gently landing at the bottom. I smiled at the onlookers.

I made my way to a nearby phone booth and called Salvador.

"I'm sending a car for you," he said.

"Wait, give me a hour or so head start. Raul must have an informant at the station—someone is tipping him off on our every move," I explained.

"Tipping him off," he repeated. "Who did you say told you about Lindavista?" he asked.

"Let's just say, a Higher Power," I responded.

"Praise God!" He laughed. "You are a very resourceful girl." He gave me accolades.

"No, not this time, Salvador, this time I'm just following His lead."

"Very well." Salvador did not question me further. "I'll do as you wish. *Vaya con dios*," he said.

I walked down that street with meticulous enthusiasm. I could not afford to miss my objective. With unwavering

CONFRONTATION

anticipation, triumphantly, I found the house, just as He described it. No garden. The lawn had been ripped out and interlock replaced it. A common practice; due to the arid climate, a garden was just too much work. I approached the house and looked in the front window. There she was, sleeping like an angel, in a room that faced the front window of the tiny house. I called her name. She sat up out of bed.

"Mommy," she answered, looking around, not realizing that my voice came from outside her window.

Tiffany jumped out of bed and ran over to the barred window, and squeezed her hands through the barrier to touch me.

"Mommy! Mommy! You're here! You found me! I was wondering if you were *ever* coming for me!" she cried.

"My baby, Mommy has been looking for you from the moment you left." I began to cry too.

"Daddy said that I had to go with him...to teach you... that you have to come back to Mexico...are you coming back now, Mommy? Did you learn your lesson?"

"Oh, I think that we have all learned something, my sweet angel," I answered softly.

The phone rang from the other room and even through the walls the sound of Raul's voice sent a chill up my spine.

"They know where I am again!!" He was angry. "How is that possible...how much time before they get here?" he questioned the informant and then hung up abruptly and called to Tiffany to get out of bed as he entered the room.

"Tiffany we have to go...fast, fast, hurry..." Raul opened the door of that stifling room and was shocked to see me standing on the other side of the barred window. Our eyes met and the maudlin moment, the much-anticipated confrontation, was void of any conversation.

I shook my head disapprovingly at him, without anger, without hostility.

I stood staring at my monster, larger than life.

What felt like an eternity of silence was interrupted by the police that Salvador had sent, banging on the door. Raul reluctantly opened the front door. I ran over and road the virtuous wave into the house, finally embracing my baby. Sweet gift from God, we had found her. It was over.

* * *

Tiffany sat on my lap as the Federales reviewed Raul's documentation. Her frail arms wrapped tightly around my neck. The chief approached me with disdain.

"I'm afraid he has been awarded custody of the child," he explained. "We cannot take her until a higher judge reverses this order." He looked me in the eye as he spoke to me.

I began to feel nausea. I pressed my face against her ear and whispered, "Don't worry, it will all be over soon."

It took everything inside of me to walk away from that house without Tiffany. I had felt so much joy, so close to God, so ready to do His will. My determination was the size of those mountains and nothing in this world was going to keep me from His promise.

Back at Salvador's factory we discussed my options, or lack of them.

"You know that you will win that appeal, I have the very best lawyers in Mexico." He lit up a cigarette and nodded his head.

"How long would that take?" I asked.

"My dear...in Mexico this could be years." He spoke truthfully.

"That's not an option. There is a young boy who will surely perish without her," I declared.

"This situation is detrimental to both my children. I

made a promise to end it."

Salvador lit another cigarette; he could see the conviction in my eyes. "Well then…" His eyes followed the smoke as it rode. "We must just…*take* her back."

For God hath not given us the spirit of fear; but of power, and of love, and of a sound mind.
—*II Timothy 1:7*

10

ALL OF THE GRACE AND ALL OF THE GLORY

That morning was glorious; it felt like I had spent most of that night in prayer and mediation. I had a plan. I duct-taped my documents, passports, and plane tickets to my bare skin, put on my pretty flowing white linen dress. Carefully hidden beneath my clothes, at the top of my thigh, was a tiny silver pistol, a gift from Salvador, "just in case." I walked down the street admiring the fragrant, vibrant pink roses that grew along the walkways of that privileged neighborhood. A nearby church's bells marked the hour. The musicality of the echoing chimes filled my heart; I lifted my face to the dessert sun and felt entirely embraced by the moment.

A passing taxi took me to my destination, a popular restaurant that Raul was fond of. He had, reluctantly, agreed to meet me for lunch, and bring Tiffany...I reminded him that it was me, ultimately, that he wanted back.

Las Fuentes, a charming but oversized buffet—with its fountains of angels, abundance of foliage, and constant bustle, it seemed like the perfect location for my maneuver.

We greeted each other cordially and Raul wasted no time before he started flirting with me. I smiled and nodded at every word he muttered. A perfect date. I imagine that he started to feel confident that all of his plans had finally come to fruition.

With immaculate timing, three voluptuous young ladies, in scant attire, approached our table to incite a conversation. They portrayed themselves as fans. Raul was delighted.

As planned, I used the distraction to excuse myself and take my daughter to the ladies room. Making eye contact with Raul, I insinuated that he should keep an eye on my bag.

I placed my oversized purse on the table as a decoy, giving him a false sense of security.

"Wait a minute!" Raul sounded panicked.

"We will be right back," I said ever so softly and took Tiffany's hand while motioning to the purse that I left behind.

We smoothly strode right pass the ladies' room and into the parking lot...

"Where are you going?" His voice startled me.

I thought of a lie.

"I thought that...I saw my friend Andreana. I was just going to say hi," I said calmly, but I knew that he didn't believe me, that any possible trust was now shattered and I would never get the opportunity to try this again.

"Get back inside!" he demanded and turned away in outrage.

As Raul turned and walked back into the restaurant, he made the blessed error of walking in front of me instead of behind, where he could see me.

My nostrils flared, I flashed my fangs and viciously scooped up my daughter, running like a deranged fiend into the street, across and deep into the parking lot, where one of Salvador's drivers was supposed to be waiting for me in a white car.

The bright dessert sunshine reflected off the roofs and hoods of every car. I could not see the white car—they all looked white! It was like staring into the sun; I was lost amidst the chaos...

"Dear Lord, help us!" I exclaimed in panic.

At a distance I could see the driver waving a baseball hat at me. I bolted for the car and threw Tiffany in the back seat. As I closed the door behind me I felt Raul's hot breath on my back. He reached for the door handle and I reached for my pistol.

"Don't do it!" I ordered, pointing the silver pistol right at him.

"Just let go of the door and walk away. It's over!" I stated with unwavering confidence.

We sped out of the lot and on down the highway toward the airport, closely followed by Raul and his brother, who was also waiting in a car in case something went wrong. They recklessly pulled up beside us and Raul started shouting profanities.

"*Hija de la chigada!*" he yelled, pulling out a gun and shooting at our car!

Jorge the driver seemed unfazed by the violence. "You get down now, girls," he said reassuringly. "Let Uncle Jorge take care of you." Jorge's demeanor had a fierce quality of a female mountain cat protecting her cubs.

Tiffany was justifiably hysterical; I did my best to calm her.

Jorge took an unexpected ramp off the highway, losing our assailant.

"Highway to Puebla?" I ask.

"Si Señora, they will be at the airport in Guadalajara," he explained.

I looked back at Tiffany—she had cried herself to sleep, her innocent face resting on a pile of clothes. I took a deep breath and inhaled the serenity. After a four-hour drive, we arrived at a private airport just outside the historical city of Puebla. An eight-seater aircraft was waiting to take us to our next destination. I bid Don Jorge goodbye and thanked him for his heroic roll in our escape.

I carried my little girl from the car to the plane. She was

visible fatigued from the emotion of the ordeal. We boarded the tiny aircraft with anticipation. Carefully, I fastened Tiffany's seat belt for her. I couldn't stop kissing her beautiful face; we smiled at each other. She seemed in good spirits. We chatted about our time apart, her baby brother, and we tried to laugh, but we both knew that it was not over yet.

Monterey would be our next destination. The Northern Sultan, with its four million inhabitants, is just south of the U.S. border. From there, you could take a flight to any city in America.

After a smooth touchdown in the industrial city, we disembarked and headed for the washroom to freshen up.

"Where are we going next, Mommy?" Her face lit up with intrigue.

"How about I let you choose," I said with excitement.

We stood in front of the information screens and watch the cities listed as if they were movie theater choices. I read them out loud. "Los Angles at 9:30, we could catch that," I said openly.

"Oh, Dallas–Fortworth at 10:45! That's closer to Toronto!" Tiffany says with excitement. We stood there for a few minutes trying to decide when a police officer interrupted our conversation abruptly.

"Excuse me, are you going to Toronto?" He spoke in Spanish.

"Oh, I'm sorry, I don't speak Spanish," I lied through my teeth.

"We are looking for a woman and child going to Toronto," he said in English. "What is your name?" he questioned me.

"My name is Cathy," I smiled flirtatiously. "Cathy Le Blanc, from Houston." Imitating a Texas drawl, I touched his shoulder and extended my hand. "And you are?" I said graciously, a true southern belle.

He looked confused.

"I wish I could help but it's getting late. Come, Jessica!" I motioned to Tiffany and she followed my lead.

"You all have yourself a lovely evening, we have to leave now but it was so very nice to meet you, good luck with that..." I continued to smile and talk, a gift that I've honed over the years. If I kept chatting, maybe he wouldn't ask me any more questions.

I praised God that they sent someone who was so naïve as not to ask for our passports.

The blessings rained down upon us like a sweet summer shower.

We headed for the main doors of the airport and exited quickly. Change of plans, no flight out from Monterey. Of course, they we looking for me.

We hopped in a cab and headed for the bus depot; there, we had two choices. We could take the nice express bus into Laredo, Texas, or take the modest "locals" bus to Nuevo Laredo just south of the U.S. border. If we boarded the first bus we would have to go through customs in Mexico. If the advisory was national, which I already witnessed in Monterrey, the authorities would surely catch us. I purchased tickets for local bus, then took a moment to call my mother.

"You have her!" she shouted with excitement.

"We are on our way to Texas. I'll call you when we are in the clear," I whispered, aware that people would be looking for us everywhere.

"How are you going to get across the border? What if you get caught!" Mother was concerned.

"Just pray for us, Mama," I said.

With the grace of a hummingbird we fled silently across the miles, down the Pan-American Highway. Vigilantly, I watched for anyone approaching us. We arrived at the slum-filled border town of Nuevo Laredo. We jumped off the bus and immediately into a taxi. The driver turned to take a good look at me and my child; he summed us up enough to trust that I would be able to pay for the exuberant ride that I had just requested.

"To the border it is, Señora!" He announced.

We sailed right by the Mexican customs and immigration, over the Rio Grande, and stopped on the American side.

"Passports, please," the border official requested.

He looked at our photos and recognized Tiffany immediately as a missing child.

"My Lord!" An out-of-character smile filled his weathered face. "There are a lot of people looking for you, young lady." He was still smiling as he walked away with our papers.

For a brief moment I thought that he wasn't going to let us in—perhaps he needed to notify someone or something like that. I felt the heat coming up off my face and red around my ears. *Please don't send us back into Mexico, please,* I prayed.

For a tense, silent moment I sat there staring at the American flag. The proverbial ribbon of my finish line. The horrendous nightmares all behind me now, I was so close, so close.

When he returned, still with a smile on his face, and passed the documents back to me, I took a deep sigh.

"So where you all headed to now?" he asked kindly.

"We're going to find a hotel for the night and fly up to Toronto tomorrow," I answered.

"There is a Holiday Inn just a few miles up the road." He motioned us through. "Welcome to The United States of America and God Bless!" he added patriotically.

I paid the taxi driver a hefty fare and thanked him for trusting us enough to take us all that way. It was after 3:00 am and our journey had left us both completely exhausted. At the front desk the clerk turned us away—no room at the Holiday Inn either. He politely explained directions to the closest hotel and pointed up the highway. A half hour into our walk I realized that it was not as close as he said it was; he assumed that we were driving. I took off my shoes and picked Tiffany up in my arms. The dry dusty wind from the highway was blowing my white dress up in the air, also getting in my eyes, making it hard to see the tiny lights of our destination. A car pulled up beside us and instead of feeling grateful I am mortified...

Three men in a modified lowrider followed us slowly, shouting and whistling at me. I was so vulnerable. I knew that I was in emanate danger. *They might rape us both and leave us to die out here.* My prayer was a simple one.

You didn't bring us all this way for it to end like this... deliver us from evil, deliver us from evil...Lord hear my prayer...

A timely local ambulance drove down the opposite side of the highway. I recklessly leaped out in front of it and motioned for them to stop. They abided.

"Are you all all right?" the driver questioned me.

"We need a ride to the hotel," I pleaded.

"Happy to help." He looked over at the car of Chicano thugs with disgust.

With the sweet grace of God, we landed in a safe hotel room, thousands of miles under our feet and eternal gratefulness on our lips.

* * *

And Jesus said unto them, "If ye have faith as a grain of mustard seed, ye shall say unto this mountain, Remove hence to younder place; and it shall remove; and nothing shall be impossible to you."
—*Romans 1:17*

* * *

In the waiting area of Toronto International airport a small jubilant crowd of well-wishers, friends, and family awaited our arrival, balloons, flowers, and teddy bears in hand. We stepped though the glass doors into full-blown cheers from the people.

Tiffany ran straight into her brother's arms!

"I'm sorry...Daddy wouldn't let me take you with us. I tried." She held his cheeks with her fragile hands.

"I missed you so much...you don't even know..." His eyes welled up and he began to cry. Tiffany wiped her brother's tears with her hands.

"Cars, you know what?" She paused. "Sometimes...if I listened very hard...I could hear you calling my name..." Then she started to cry.

"That's because I was," he smiled.

Not a dry eye in the crowd—even strangers could feel that something very special had taken place here.

Seeing my two children reunited after more than a year of uncertainty and heartache was the absolute testimony of pure divine intervention.

"You did it, Mommy! You really did it! You kept your promise!" He laughed and cried simultaneously.

I smiled and nodded. The emotion of the illustrious moment and the magnitude of my journey had left me speechless.

Now *that's* a Miracle!

* * *

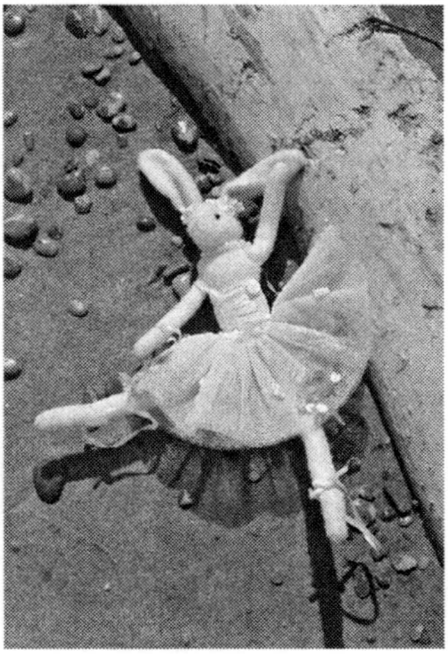

AUTHOR'S BIO

At seventeen years old, this Latin-Canadian was living in Acapulco, Mexico with her mother, a professional dancer, and three sisters, first dancing with Jerry Jackson Ballet at the Acapulco Princess Hotel. Years later in Mexico City, while performing on the weekly television show *Siempre en Domingo* as a dancer with young Ricky Martin and Latin heartthrob Luis Miguel, Annamaria was discovered by an American photographer who launched her into the modeling industry. Soon her face graced billboards from Tijuana to Tampico, endorsing such name brands as Adidas, David Aaron, Hanes, and Pepsi.

Annamaria Sparks lives the life of a dancer, model, actress, and artist, and is now happily re-married to the light of her life. She thanks God for the many blessings.

* * *

*A man is not measured by his wealth but by his good deeds;
let all humanitarians be always remembered.*

* * *

A very special thanks to these good people:
Christine Banville, Linda Harper, David Eisenstat
The Keg Spirit Foundation
Child Find Ontario
Detective Denis Le Plant, Sergeant David Ground
The York Regional Police Department
Aaron Litchi
Bension Sadez
Reverend Cory Millben
All the wonderful people of Grant A.M.E. Church
The Talent of Mill City Press